SHIFT
POINTS

SHIFT POINTS

ONE HUNDRED IDEAS TO

SHIFT YOUR ORGANIZATION

INTO TOP GEAR

DAVE RAMOS

Advantage®

Published by Advantage, Charleston, South Carolina.
Member of Advantage Media Group.

ADVANTAGE is a registered trademark and the Advantage colophon is a trademark of Advantage Media Group, Inc.

Shiftpoints® is a registered trademark and the Shiftpoints Logo is a trademark of Shiftpoints, Inc.

Printed in the United States of America.

ISBN: 978-159932-448-7
LCCN: 2013949751

This publication is designed to provide accurate and authoritative information in regard to the subject matter covered. It is sold with the understanding that the publisher is not engaged in rendering legal, accounting, or other professional services. If legal advice or other expert assistance is required, the services of a competent professional person should be sought.

Advantage Media Group is proud to be a part of the Tree Neutral® program. Tree Neutral offsets the number of trees consumed in the production and printing of this book by taking proactive steps such as planting trees in direct proportion to the number of trees used to print books. To learn more about Tree Neutral, please visit **www.treeneutral.com**. To learn more about Advantage's commitment to being a responsible steward of the environment, please visit **www.advantagefamily.com/green**.

Advantage Media Group is a publisher of business, self-improvement, and professional development books and online learning. We help entrepreneurs, business leaders, and professionals share their Stories, Passion, and Knowledge to help others Learn & Grow. Do you have a manuscript or book idea that you would like us to consider for publishing? Please visit **advantagefamily.com** or call 1.866.775.1696.

INTELLECTUAL PROPERTY

SHIFTPOINTS® is a registered trademark of SHIFT-POINTS Inc., a strategy and organizational development consultancy based in Tysons Corner, VA.

The SHIFTPOINTS logo is a trademark of SHIFT-POINTS Inc., a strategy and organizational development consultancy based in Tysons Corner VA.

The following terms are trademarks of SHIFTPOINTS Inc.:

- Decide One Thing™
- Decide One Thing. Align Everything. Win!™
- The Seven Accelerators™

CONTENTS

INTRODUCTION:

WHEN YOU HIT REDLINE,

IT IS TIME TO SHIFT

Starting a company is a lot like starting a car. You need a lot of energy. To get moving, you need to be in first gear.

In a car, you can go from zero to 60 mph in just a few seconds.

In business, you can go from zero to your first million in just a few years...or months. It can be exhilarating... making progress, closing sales, building a team...you did it!

Pretty soon, everyone is working at a frantic pace. It is literally impossible to work harder, and you wonder if you can even keep up the current rate. But in spite of your efforts, growth has plateaued.

The business has redlined.

The first step is to identify why you have redlined.

Is it your strategy? Your executive team? Your product? Your capital? All of the above?

Next, you must design the strategic change and shift the organization to the next gear.

At this stage, fear sets in because shifting gears is risky. What if you stall the business? What if people resist the changes? What if the new executives don't work out?

Gas pedal out…clutch pedal in…shift into second… clutch pedal out…gas pedal in.

Eventually, however, you must accept the risk, plot the course, and make the change.

Because what got you here won't get you there.

SHIFTPOINTS developed a model to help organizations drive strategic change, called the Seven Accelerators™.

The process starts with what we call Decide One Thing™. This helps organizations identify their one defining differentiation.

We then use your One Thing to align everything—and everyone.

The process works.

Since implementing the Seven Accelerators, clients have doubled, tripled, and even quadrupled their revenue.

Decide One Thing. Align Everything. Win!™

DECIDE ONE THING

DECIDE ONE THING

Every organization thinks it is unique.

But most are actually vanilla and undifferentiated.

In contrast, high performers decide to become incredibly, fanatically great at One Thing, which gives them a unique, compelling, and differentiating identity.

Walmart chose price as its One Thing. Nordstrom chose customer service. Apple chose product design. Dell chose customization. BMW chose performance. Lexus chose quality.

High-performance organizations recognize that they can't be great at 27 things. They have to pick one.

Deciding One Thing is about planting your flag and declaring your differentiation. It is the starting point for building a differentiation-driven organization.

And of course, Deciding One Thing is not just words. Differentiation-driven organizations are relentless, uncompromising, and unwavering about becoming great at their One Thing … and that's why they win.

So, what's the One Thing that differentiates you?

THE STARTING POINT

Whenever I meet a new executive, I always start with the same question, "How do you differentiate your firm?" You'd be surprised how many people can't answer that question.

These organizations look alike, sound alike, and act alike. Their products are the same. Their brand blends in.

They disappear into a bland vanilla sea of sameness.

Creating a real and meaningful differentiation is extremely difficult.

The SHIFTPOINTS model is that organizations must be good at many things...but the way to win is to become *differentiatingly great* at One Thing.

Our first book, *Decide One Thing,* made a clear and compelling case for this idea. We examined a wide variety of organizations who have applied it, from iconic brands such as BMW, Nordstrom, and Dyson, to high-growth innovators such as SiteOrganic, BTI360, and NeoSystems.

So, is your organization *differentiatingly great* at One Thing? If not, perhaps you should pick up a copy of *Decide One Thing.*

THE ONE THING THAT'S MISSING

Many organizations have vision statements, mission statements, and core values. When reviewing these, we often find them to be boring and uninspiring.

The One Thing they are missing is a defining differentiation.

This is why we advise clients to lock down their defining differentiation *first.*

To decide what your defining differentiation (your One Thing) is, complete this sentence: "We are good at lots of things, but we are differentiatingly great at

_____."

My *Decide One Thing* book lays out a comprehensive methodology to help executive teams make this decision.

Once you have decided your One Thing, the vision statement, mission statement, and core values can be written with precision and clarity.

PS: I have never seen an organization that was transformed because it spent six months wordsmithing its vision, mission, and values.

In contrast, organizations that have fully applied our **Decide One Thing. Align Everything. Win!** model have indeed been radically transformed.

CLONING

I started my career at IBM.

Shortly after I joined the company, we launched the first IBM PC. IBM was not first to market but soon set the standard for what a PC would become.

Soon afterward, competitors began selling what became known as "IBM clones." These products had similar specifications but were sold at a 20 percent or more discount from IBM.

In virtually every market, followers will copy, reverse engineer, or clone your best ideas.

Some will even downright steal them. (Apple and Samsung are fighting a huge battle in court over this very issue.)

However, everyone knows who the true leader is. And being the leader, that company is always One Step Ahead.

Leaders maintain their leadership by staying intensely focused on their One Thing.

Refining critical processes—their One Way—to world-class levels leads to the creation of a differentiating competitive advantage.

WHO ARE YOU?

When you meet people, they often ask, "What do you do?" But what they are really asking is, "Who are you?"

This is the existential question.

It is very hard for people to answer these questions for themselves. But it is even harder for organizations to answer them since the question is not "Who am I?" but "Who are we?"

Obviously, organizations don't want to say, "We are the same as everyone else."

The ideal answer describes what makes you uniquely you. This requires your organization, which is comprised of a group of unrelated and disparate people, to find a "familial DNA marker."

The answers must reflect both the present—who you really are, and the future—who you aspire to be.

It all starts when you Decide One Thing.

ONE HUNDRED THINGS

I know what you are thinking. For years, we have been advocating that clients "Decide One Thing."

Now, we have One Hundred Things?

In order to become differentiatingly great at your One Thing, you will have to improve hundreds of things.

Imagine that you wanted to transform a Honda Accord into a world-class racecar. You would not just improve one thing...you would improve hundreds of things!

In a racecar, you find speed in hundreds of small places: a tweak to the tire pressure, one turn of the front wing, one new part that reduces the weight of the car by a few grams.

Race teams are obsessive about all of these details. They have to be, since the difference between winning and losing is often less than one second.

Likewise, leaders of high-performance organizations are obsessive about the details. They find improved performance in hundreds of small places.

All of the pieces of a high-performance racecar are dynamically interconnected. Just like a high-performance organization.

DECIDE ONE THING. ALIGN EVERYTHING. WIN!

The starting point is the decision to become differentiatingly great at One Thing.

You can't just Decide One Thing, you have to Align Everything!

The SHIFTPOINTS model is to use an organization's One Thing as a catalyst for driving organizational change and alignment.

And when we say "everything," we really do mean everything, from your corporate description to your job descriptions.

Sales proposals to invoices.

On-boarding to off-boarding.

Website to jobsite.

That is why we call it "100 Points of Alignment."

ACCELERATOR #2

DEFINE ONE IDENTITY

DEFINE ONE IDENTITY

Every organization has an identity.

But most are bland and boring.

In contrast, high performers leverage their One Thing to create a brand identity that is unique and differentiating.

Most think a brand identity is a logo. However, it includes dozens of components, including your mission, vision, values, culture, color scheme, brand vibe, naming conventions, and more.

In addition, your identity extends into human resources, since people are "the personification of the brand."

Every organization has dozens of competitors—or more! Defining One Identity will allow you to occupy a clear market position, create customer mindshare, and attract people who share your DNA.

So, does your organization have a differentiating identity?

SMART VISION

In high-performance organizations, the vision is far more than a traditional vision statement, most of which are just meaningless blah-blah-blah. It is a "SMART Vision," which has two components:

- One specific measurable goal. This provides high performers with a way to define success. Many goals are captured in catchy, memorable phrases, such as "$25M by 2025."

- Visionary language that inspires and connects with people on an emotional level.

This combines science and art. It appeals to both right and left brain types. It is specific enough to provide direction and inspiring enough to motivate people to achieve it.

A recent trip to the eye doctor reminded me just how rare 20/20 vision is. Only 35 percent of all adults have 20/20 vision without glasses or corrective surgery.

And according to my (admittedly unscientific) research, only 35 percent of organizations have 20/20 vision as well.

Crafting a SMART Vision might be just the correction your organization needs to see 20/20 again.

UNIQUE AND UNITED

The art of management is to find what is unique about each person. The art of leadership is to find what is common among people and unite them into a high-performance team.

An organization's DNA is made up of your unifying values.

DNA can't be seen on the balance sheet, but it is one of the organization's most valuable assets. Strong values will allow an organization to withstand a crisis and will guide leaders faced with radically complex decisions.

According to Wikipedia, a value system is "a set of consistent ethic values and measures used for the purpose of ethical or ideological integrity. A well defined value system is a moral code."

In high-performance organizations, these values become their DNA.

In high-growth organizations, teams turn into departments. Departments turn into divisions, and divisions can turn into silos. If you are not careful, the people down the hall can become the enemy.

To avoid this, every employee's DNA must share a common familial marker.

LIVING VALUES

Every organization has values. Most have even taken the time to write them down. Some even create posters.

But only a select few actually live their values.

Values are one of those soft things that many leaders struggle with. However, if you want to build a high-performance culture, you have to make them real.

Because the soft stuff is the hard stuff!

High-performance organizations are fanatical about their values.

But far too often, we see leaders who tolerate all kinds of destructive, dysfunctional behaviors that are inconsistent with the organization's values.

Such as the employee who literally described her teammates as evil.

We advise our clients to have a zero tolerance policy on this kind of behavior, especially among those in leadership positions. Confronting dysfunctional behavior is difficult, but tolerating it will destroy you.

ONE WORD

At SHIFTPOINTS, we often challenge leaders to summarize their organizations.

In One Word.

The question for you is, "If you had to summarize your organization in One Word, what would it be?"

Is there One Word that you can own? One Word that you can burn into your brand promise? One Word that you can use as your guiding North Star?

This process is extremely difficult. In most organizations, our first pass at this exercise with the executive team generates over 20 different words!

However, finding and owning One Word is an important part of the Decide One Thing process.

According to *Webster*, there are about one million words in the English vocabulary.

Surely you can find One Word that you can uniquely own.

ONE TAGLINE

Often, it is helpful to summarize your One Thing as a tagline.

And ultimately, a great tagline answers one question: Why? As in, "Why should someone choose you?"

You choose a BMW because it is the Ultimate Driving Machine.

You choose a Lexus because of their Pursuit of Perfection.

You choose Group W because they are The Right Answer.

You choose SiteOrganic because they help your website Produce Fruit.

BTI360 chose a unique approach. Their tagline highlights their passion for people. They are: Developing Ultimate Teammates.

Taglines are helpful.

But what really counts is becoming differentiatingly great at your One Thing.

Then your tagline will be a lot more than mere words. It will summarize your differentiating competitive advantage.

ONE COLOR

Building a unique and differentiating brand identity is difficult.

Surprisingly, a simple thing such as picking One Color can make a huge difference.

One of our clients, BTI360, competes in a segment with hundreds of competitors. Most of them look alike, sound alike, act alike, and blend into a sea of vanilla sameness.

During our Decide One Thing program, we learned that BTI360 was known for the orange lanyards that teammates wore to hold their badge.

I distinctly remember saying to them, "Well, if we are going to be orange, let's be orange!"

That led to a total brand transformation around their One Color. Everything at BTI360 is orange. The notebooks are orange. The walls are orange. The pens are orange. The sports drinks are orange.

Sometimes, teammates even wear orange socks!

When it came time to send flowers to a teammate's spouse, the decision about what kind of flowers to send was easy. You guessed it: orange ones.

Pick One Color, and own it. You'll never blend in again.

ONE MESSAGE

High-performance organizations stand for One Thing.

And these high performers take this one step further by delivering One Message.

This means that every element of your communications program must be aligned.

Walmart's One Thing is price, and their One Message is "Low Prices, Always." Every ad is simply produced and talks about saving money. No expensive pitchmen for Walmart. The company's mission, "Saving people money so they can live better," says it all.

Apple's One Thing is design, and their One Message is all about being cool. The store is cool. The employees are cool. Even Apple's power supplies are cool.

BMW's One Thing is performance, and their One Message is that a BMW is "The Ultimate Driving Machine." Their website even features interviews with suspension engineers.

It takes fanatical discipline to create and maintain brand alignment. The organizations that can do so are on their way to becoming iconic.

DEFINE ONE IDENTITY
AN ALIGNMENT CHECKLIST

Our *Decide One Thing. Align Everything. Win!* model provides a roadmap for creating a differentiating competitive advantage.

But it only works if you really do align everything and everyone.

Consider the following checklist as a starting point:

1. One SMART Vision
2. One DNA (core values)
3. One for All (culture)
4. One Brand Vibe
5. One Logo
6. One Tagline
7. One Color
8. One Message
9. One Story
10. One Word

If you have aligned all ten of these elements of your corporate identity, you are probably on your way to the winner's circle!

DESIGN ONE STRATEGY

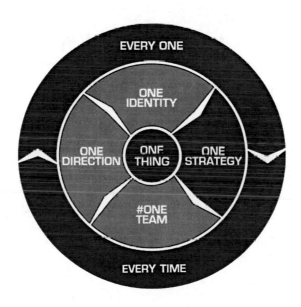

DESIGN ONE STRATEGY

Every organization has a strategy.

But most are diffused and reactionary.

In contrast, high performers Design One Strategy that is intensely focused.

They would rather dominate One Market than dabble in a dozen of them.

Walmart and Kmart started at about the same time.

Walmart stayed intensely focused on the discount retail segment, systematically reducing costs and passing the savings along to customers.

Kmart dabbled with sporting goods stores (acquiring The Sports Authority), bookstores (acquiring Borders), office products (acquiring OfficeMax), and more.

Clearly, the focused strategy was the big winner.

So, is your organization more like Walmart or Kmart?

WHERE ARE YOU GOING?

Alice in Wonderland captures a great dialog between Alice and the Cheshire Cat.

Alice asks, "Would you tell me, please, which way I ought to go from here?"

"That depends a good deal on where you want to get to," answers the Cat.

To which Alice replies, "I don't much care where."

The Cheshire Cat answers, "Then it doesn't matter which way you go."

As a dog lover, it is hard to admit that a cat could be right, but in this case, the Cheshire Cat is exactly right.

You can't develop a strategy until you know where you want to go.

READING THE SIGNS

High-performance leaders see things that others don't, and they see them before others do.

They have an uncanny knack for "reading the signs."

Some of the most common signs include:

- STOP. What should you stop doing? (Once you Decide One Thing, this should be relatively easy.)

- CURVE AHEAD. What is changing in your market? Many organizations are facing massive change in their industry.

- DEAD END. Some organizations are simply heading in the wrong direction. Their industry segment underwent a massive shift years ago, but they were not able to change.

- FORK IN THE ROAD. Some organizations are at a major decision point. They have two radically different alternatives ahead, and they have to choose.

- YIELD. In every organization, there comes a time for the leader to yield power to others. Most leaders avoid this decision.

Every leader has to read the signs. High-performance leaders read them sooner than others.

THE SEAT OF YOUR PANTS

Recently I was in Napa Valley and fulfilled a lifelong goal: to fly a glider.

Floating along like a bird at 5,000 feet above the beautiful California countryside sure puts things in perspective. No motor. No noise. Just you and 900 pounds of aluminum.

You feel everything in the seat of your pants!

And I could not help but make the connection between my flying experience and what we see in organizations.

The phrase "flying by the seat of your pants" traces back to the 1930s and was first widely used in reports of Douglas Corrigan's flight from Brooklyn to Ireland in 1938.

But the real story was that although Corrigan flew to Ireland, he had actually submitted a flight plan to fly to California. He was thereafter known as "Wrong Way Corrigan" and starred as himself in the 1938 movie *The Flying Irishman.*

And just like Wrong Way Corrigan, flying by the seat of your pants is a great way for organizations to end up in the wrong place as well.

High-performance organizations have a clear vision and a flight plan that actually will get them there.

PIPE DREAMS

I love Jim Collins, and *Good to Great* is one of the best business books ever written.

Many organizations have adopted his ideas, including the "big, hairy, audacious goal" or BHAG concept.

But too often the BHAG is really a "big, hairy audacious, delusional pipe dream."

These outrageous and totally unrealistic goals are the corporate equivalent of New Year's resolutions, easy to set, but darn near impossible to keep.

Executives think they are audacious, but their teams know they are ridiculous.

Wise leaders would rather confront them in the privacy of a hotel conference room before the BHAG is announced, than backtrack in front of a skeptical group of employees at an all-hands meeting.

DRILLING FOR OIL

Starting a company involves a crazy leap into the unknown.

We call it "drilling for oil."

In the early days of oil exploration, drilling a "wildcat" well—searching for oil in a field where it had not yet been discovered—had only a 20 percent chance of success. Thus, 80 percent were "dry holes."

Starting a company still involves a bit of wildcatting.

In the early days, entrepreneurs must cast a wide net. Assumptions must be tested. Beta products must be developed. Target markets must be validated.

Sometimes, you drill a lot of holes, looking for the big one.

When wildcatters strike oil, they halt their other explorations and focus on extracting the oil from their one winner. Entrepreneurs must do the same thing.

This is the "real enterprise" phase. This begins with locking down your One Thing and pruning the activities that don't fit.

Failure to make this transition is a root cause of plateaued growth.

IRRATIONAL PERSEVERANCE

When I started SHIFTPOINTS, I got a lot of great advice. One of the most memorable was this:

"The defining trait of a successful entrepreneur is irrational perseverance."

I now fully understand the meaning of that statement.

It means that you keep going after clients renege on contracts.

It means that you keep going after partners renege on agreements.

It means you keep going after hundreds of failures.

Successful entrepreneurs just keep going and going. And going.

In *Decide One Thing,* I shared the inspiring story of Sir James Dyson.

He built 5,127 prototypes before he invented the vacuum that "never loses suction."

Five thousand, one hundred and twenty-seven!

That's irrational perseverance!

THE WILL AND THE SKILL

Virtually every organization wants to grow. Growth is a sign of health, prosperity, and vitality.

Yet only one in a thousand companies grows from $1M to $100M in revenue (source: *Winning Performance*).

The reason: companies have the will to grow but not the skill.

Many pursue a haphazard mix of tactics.

An acquisition here.

A new market over there.

A couple of new products for good measure.

Others just try harder. They work longer hours and make more calls. They set higher quotas and demand better results.

Most of the time, these tactics create a short-term flurry of activity but not real, sustainable, and profitable growth.

Our **Decide One Thing. Align Everything. Win!** model provides a systematic approach.

If you want to be one in a thousand, perhaps this is the methodology you have been looking for.

DON'T DABBLE...DOMINATE

The worst possible strategy is to be "all things to all people."

Thus, an organization must narrow its focus. This is a lot more difficult than it sounds, because many organizations are afraid that narrowing their focus will reduce revenue and growth.

In fact, just the opposite is true.

Many entrepreneurial organizations are consumed with tactics. If they even have a strategy, it could be summarized as "more."

More markets, more proposals, more products, more cities, and so on.

The problem is that sometimes, more is less.

Entering more markets often distracts your team. As a result, you take your eye off the core business.

Writing more proposals often divides your attention. As a result, you don't have the time to design the right solution for any of them.

Developing more products often dilutes your limited R&D resources. You end up with five mediocre products rather than one market-defining flagship.

Avoid these delusions, and you will dominate!

THE MOST IMPORTANT WORD

I once worked for a leader who had a saying:

"The most important word in a leader's vocabulary is NO."

I'm not sure if that is true, but it might be a good discipline for leaders tempted to always pursue more.

High performers have the discipline to sort through all of the strategic options and focus on the few initiatives that will really produce results.

This means saying NO to lots of things, so you can indeed become differentiatingly great at One Thing.

This means saying NO to lots of good ideas, so you can focus on the Great Ones.

This means saying NO to dabbling in lots of markets, so you can Dominate One Market.

This means saying NO to good candidates, so you can hold out until you find a Great One.

Saying NO to good things, ideas, markets, and people is hard.

But it is exactly what you have to do.

STRATEGY TESTING

....

We have developed a little pop quiz, designed to test your strategy.

- Of all the strategies you could have designed, why is this strategy the best one?

- If you execute this strategy flawlessly, will you be number one in your industry?

- Do you have the resources (human and financial) to execute the strategy?

- Will this strategy improve your win rate?

- Has this strategy identified the things that you will stop doing?

- Will this strategy clearly differentiate you from your (current and future) competitors?

- Does this strategy clearly identify growth opportunities (new markets and new services)?

- Does this strategy strengthen your core business?

- Can you actually execute the strategy you have designed…or is it just wishful thinking?

Did your strategy pass the test?

CATCH THE RABBIT

There is an ancient Chinese proverb that states,

"If you chase two rabbits, both will escape."

However, the phenomenon we see far too often is not organizations that chase two rabbits, but those that chase 12 rabbits!

These organizations often have a different strategy every day.

On Monday, they are going green.

On Tuesday, they are opening an office in China.

One Wednesday, they are buying their biggest competitor.

On Thursday, they are cashing out.

By Friday, their employees can't wait for happy hour.

They want to enter every market, develop every product, and chase every deal. Their offices are a blur of activity.

Over here. No, over there. Wait, no, over there. Faster. Arghhhh!

FOCUS

In contrast, high performers are much more focused.

They have the unique ability to prioritize opportunities.

They don't want to enter every market; they want to enter the right markets, ones that they can dominate.

They don't want to develop every product; they want to develop the right products, those that can be category-defining game changers.

They don't want to chase every deal; they want to win the most profitable and strategic deals.

And they are happy to let their competitors scurry around, chasing 12 rabbits while they feast on a delicious bowl of hasenpfeffer.

Otherwise known as rabbit stew!

THE GROWTH CYCLE

In addition to the 12 rabbits problem, there is another organizational pathology that we see all the time.

We call it the under/over problem.

The under/over problem follows a predictable progression.

Organizations tend to *underestimate* the time, cost, competitive entrenchment, and complexity of entering new markets.

Organizations tend to *overestimate* their own capabilities, especially in terms of the organization's ability to change, create new products, or enter new markets. Leaders often just pile more work onto the existing staff and expect them to fit it in somehow.

The result of both *underestimating* costs and *overestimating* capabilities leads organizations to do too many things at once. Rather than focus on the best opportunity, they go after all of them.

This dilutes resources and leads to a phenomenon of *underinvesting* in each of the growth initiatives.

None of them have enough critical mass to succeed.

Thus, none of the growth initiatives succeed. The results are decidedly *underwhelming!*

YOU CAN'T SELL WHAT
YOU HAVE NOT BOUGHT!

In order to effectively sell their employees on the organization's strategy, executives must have fully bought in to it. Why?

Because you can't sell what you have not bought.

And buying something—anything—involves a predictable process.

You must be aware of the strategy. It sounds stupid, but many employees are not even aware that the organization has a strategy.

You must be convinced that the strategy is right, and that it will work.

You must be convinced that it is the best one the organization could have chosen.

You must be convinced that it will help the organization win.

You must personally buy in to the benefits of the strategy for *yourself.*

Only when executives have fully bought in will they be able to sell other people on buying in as well.

As Zig Ziglar said, "You can't be convincing if you are not convinced."

INVEST ONE DAY

SHIFTPOINTS works with what we call "Fast Lane Leaders."

Most have short attention spans and are highly tactical in their thinking.

This is fine when the business is small, but it is a root cause of plateaued growth, disengaged employees, dissatisfied customers, and disgruntled investors.

Therefore, we recommend that executive teams invest One Day/Quarter on their strategy. This includes four critical tasks:

- Reviewing the results from the last quarter
- Refining the strategy based on new developments
- Developing 90-day sprint initiatives
- Launching the plan in an all-hands meeting/call

This One Day/Quarter strategic planning cadence creates an organization that is both highly aligned and highly agile.

STRATEGICALLY TACTICAL

Many entrepreneurial organizations are so tactical that their long-term plan covers what to do after lunch!

The goal of our Invest One Day approach is to create a new kind of operating model.

We call it strategically tactical.

First, *strategically tactical* organizations have a clearly articulated long-term vision. This provides everyone with much-needed directional clarity and stability.

Second, *strategically tactical* organizations use a strategy development process that is dynamic and agile.

We recommend the 90-day model, where strategies are refined, aligned, and communicated every 90 days.

Finally, *strategically tactical* organizations translate their strategies into tactics that drive results every day.

DESIGN ONE STRATEGY
AN ALIGNMENT CHECKLIST

Our **Decide One Thing. Align Everything. Win!** model provides a roadmap for creating a differentiating competitive advantage.

But it only works if you really do align everything and everyone.

Consider the following checklist as a starting point:

1. One Target

2. One Portfolio

3. One Flagship

4. One World

5. One Price Point

6. One (business) Model

7. One EcoSystem (partners)

8. One Way

9. One Discipline (pruning)

10. One Benchmark (competition)

If you have aligned all ten of these elements of your corporate strategy, you are probably on your way to the winner's circle!

DEVELOP THE
#ONE TEAM

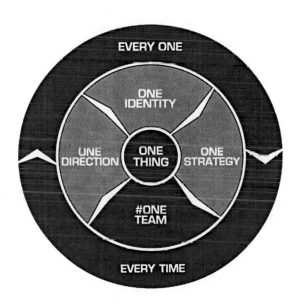

DEVELOP THE #ONE TEAM

Every organization, by definition, has an organization.

But most are pretty dysfunctional.

In contrast, high performers develop their people into the #One Team in the industry.

Developing the #One Team will take an investment of both time and money, but it will yield an incredible return.

High performers are very intentional about organizational development. They create an environment that attracts the very best people.

They engage and inspire them to do their very best work. And they create a system that aligns the strengths of every person to accomplish extraordinary things.

Building the #One Team in your industry starts with the senior leaders.

Jim Collins made "getting the right people on the bus" part of our lexicon. But often, the real issue is aligning the bus drivers to work as One Team.

So, do you have the #One Team in your industry?

BUS DRIVERS

Many organizations talk about getting the right people on the bus.

Getting the right people on the bus is good. But to be truly great, you must have the right people driving the bus.

Driving a bus is a specialized skill.

In most states, bus drivers are required to have a special commercial driver's license.

Since the stakes are high—bus drivers have other people's lives in their hands—they need special training.

It can take years to fully master the trade.

Likewise, leading an organization is a specialized skill. Leaders have other people's lives—and livelihoods—in their hands.

If you want to build a high-performance organization, you have to start at the top—with the bus drivers.

"EXECUTIVE GRADE"

GMC Trucks has an advertising slogan, "We are professional grade." (A great brand position, by the way.)

Building a high-performance organization requires high-performance executives who demonstrate a rare mix of skills, abilities, and behaviors.

These leaders are "executive grade."

So, what makes a leader executive grade? There are several characteristics we look for:

- Executive grade results
- Executive grade strategic thinking
- Executive grade perspective
- Executive grade expertise
- Executive grade communications

Every one of our clients is focused on building a high-performance executive team.

Often, they ask us to help evaluate potential candidates. We always give them the same advice:

You must have "A-Players in C-Roles."

A LEADER WORTH FOLLOWING

Every year, millions of people celebrate Easter.

They go to church to worship Jesus and celebrate the good news of His resurrection. They proclaim Him as Lord and pledge their allegiance as followers.

To millions, He is a leader worth following.

So, how about you? Are <u>you</u> a leader worth following?

Leaders, by definition, have followers. The question for you to consider is, "*Why* are they following?"

Are they following because they have to? After all, you're the boss. Or, are they following because they want to, because they believe in you, in your vision, and in your strategy?

What makes you a leader worth following?

All leaders should examine themselves and ponder another question: "Why *should* people follow me?"

And the answer needs to be something more compelling than "because I'm the boss."

EXECUTIVES SET THE BAR

Jean-Baptiste Karr, the French journalist and satirist, first penned the phrase, "Plus ça change, plus c'est la même chose," which is loosely translated as "The more things change, the more they stay the same."

In organizations, the phenomenon I observe most is executives who give lip service to change but in reality never change.

Thus, paraphrasing Monsieur Karr:

"The less executives change, the more the organization will stay the same."

In most cases, the chief executive is the most bought-in person in the organization. After all, they designed the strategy and goals in the first place.

But the big problem with buy-in is that it "leaks."

Based on our research, the executive team in most organizations is 10–30 percent less bought-in than the chief executive.

In addition, employees are 10–30 percent less bought-in than the senior executives they report to. This can lead to a 50 percent gap between the CEO and the employees.

Closing this gap will require everyone to change.

MAGNIFICATION

Senior executives' actions (good or bad) are magnified and replicated disproportionately by the rest of the organization.

If the senior executives work well together as a team, the organization will be a consistent top performer.

If the senior executives have a common vision, the organization will align behind it.

If the senior executives articulate a clear and compelling strategy, the organization will execute and deliver it.

If the senior executives send mixed messages, the organization will shift into neutral.

If the senior executive team is a little dysfunctional, the organization will be very dysfunctional.

If they are very dysfunctional, the organization will be a disaster.

So, if you want to improve the performance of your organization, start at the top.

WORDS AND DEEDS

One of the root causes of disengaged employees is what we call "organizational hypocrisy," in which organizations say one thing but do another.

Unfortunately, this pathology is discouragingly common.

Leaders say that employees are their greatest asset but axe them without reservation as soon as the economy sours.

Leaders say that the customer is number one, but don't confront the brutal facts about their delivery performance issues because fixing the problem will cost too much.

Organizations proclaim their core values, but the resource allocation decisions contradict them.

The recruiting brochure says that the organization values diversity, but it has six old white guys in the boardroom.

They preach excellence, but practice mediocrity.

Frankly, employees in this kind of organization are rightfully cynical. They have witnessed so much dysfunctional behavior that they tune out. The words are just executive blah-blah-blah.

WE BEFORE ME

Jon Katzenbach, in his well-researched book *Teams at the Top*, differentiates between "single-leader working groups" and "performance driven teams."

And in my experience, we need a third category: "Dysfunctional, destructive groups."

In these groups, the sum is less than the parts.

Too often, the most dysfunctional team in an organization is the executive team. In fact, the employee engagement research suggests that most employees do not trust their executives to do the right thing (see "The Trust Gap").

These "dysfunctional, destructive groups" are characterized by low team trust, infighting, back-stabbing, and undermining. And that's on a good day!

In contrast, high-performance executive teams put "we before me." As a result, the sum total impact is *far greater* than the abilities of each individual executive.

Call it high-performance executive team math.

ALL FOR ONE

The Three Musketeers is a novel by Alexandre Dumas that is set in seventeenth-century Paris. It tells the story of a young man named d'Artagnan who wants to join the Musketeers of the Guard.

The Three Musketeers made the phrase "All for one, and one for all" famous ("Tous pour un, et un pour tous").

Unfortunately, the dynamic we often see among executive teams is:

"All for me and none for you."

Sometimes this behavior is demonstrated during the budgeting process, which creates a zero-sum game.

Sometimes, it is demonstrated in unhealthy internal competition.

The enemy can't be down the hall!

We once worked with an organization where every executive had his or her own compensation plan, and none of the compensation was tied to the overall corporate performance.

You can guess what that place was like.

THE REAR VIEW MIRROR

One of my favorite movies is *The Gumball Rally,* a 1976 comedy inspired by the actual Cannonball Baker Sea-to-Shining-Sea Memorial Trophy Dash held by Brock Yates.

In the movie, the Ferrari team hires a professional racecar driver, played by Raul Julia, to give it a competitive advantage. The first thing he does is tear off the rearview mirror and toss it out of the car.

He then utters a line with many leadership implications (it helps to use big hand gestures when reading this):

"The first-ah rule-ah of Italian-ah driving is … what's-ah behind-ah me is not important."

And having driven in Italy, I can tell you first-hand that many Italian drivers still apply this rule!

The corollary for leaders is not what's behind you, but *who*. And unlike racing, in organizations, who is behind you is very important.

Great leaders inspire people to follow them. They demonstrate a real, genuine appreciation for the unique talents of everyone on the team. These leaders tailor their style to each person's unique temperament.

Maybe the place to start is a long, considerate look at the people in your rearview mirror.

"BUT HE HAS NOTHING ON!"

Perhaps one of the greatest management lessons ever written was *The Emperor's New Clothes* by Hans Christian Andersen.

You know the story.

The king buys a new, custom-made suit from two swindlers posing as weavers. The suit was to be made of a material that "possessed the wonderful quality of being invisible to any man who was unfit for his office or unpardonably stupid."

Although it is a sham, everyone is afraid to admit it, for fear that they themselves would look stupid. Even worse, they are afraid to tell the king.

Only a little child breaks the chain of self-deception:

"But he has nothing on!"

Even then, the king refuses to listen.

While some "emperor's new clothes" behavior is a natural result of deference to the leader's rank, many leaders exacerbate the problem.

In contrast, high-performance leaders go out of their way to get to the real truth.

Of course, you must have thick skin. If you ask for the truth, some people will actually give it to you.

FOLLOW THE LEADER

Have you ever tried to follow someone who didn't know where they were going?

27 U-turns and a few near-misses later, you finally arrive at your destination.

Far too many employees are trying to follow leaders who simply don't know where they are going. The employees are willing to follow, even willing to go the extra mile, but eventually give up because it is too frustrating.

You can't follow a leader who is lost.

Deciding where to go in uncertain times is tough.

Often, a road that looks promising turns out to be a dead end. Sometimes, the organization is faced with a major "fork in the road" decision.

As Yogi Berra famously said, "When you get to a fork in the road, take it!"

So, how do you plot a course in uncertain times?

Having a locked-down defining differentiation can provide the long-term strategic clarity you need.

And if you aren't really sure where to go, perhaps it is time to stop and ask for directions.

PRONOUNS

I went to a crummy high school, and grammar was definitely not my thing.

In fact, I probably did not learn what a pronoun was until I worked at AnswerLogic. (At AnswerLogic, I also learned that marketing is a gerund—who knew?)

However, I have now decided that pronouns play a surprisingly important part in building a high-performance organization.

When employees—*especially executives*—talk, I listen for their choice of pronoun.

- Do they say, "When they decided," or "When we decided?"

- Do they say, "Their strategy is to…" or "Our strategy is to…"

- Do they say, "Their goals are…" or "My goals are…"

So leaders, start listening for the pronouns everyone is using.

You can't finish in first place if everyone talks in the third person.

MANAGEMENT BY BESTSELLER

Ken Blanchard is a legendary management thinker and author. So is Jim Collins. And John Kotter. And Warren Bennis. And Marcus Buckingham. And so are hundreds of others.

Great leaders are always learning, and reading great books is important.

However, trying to implement the ideas from every book you read can unwittingly increase misalignment, creating a phenomenon that one of our associates calls,

Management by bestseller.

This kind of herky-jerky leadership makes employees reach for the barf bags!

Often, this comes from the top. Every time the CEO reads a new book or attends a new seminar, there is a new initiative.

Rather than making a long-term commitment to one initiative, these CEOs have "one night stands" with all of them.

It would be far better to pick One Book—perhaps this one—and make a long-term strategic commitment to the methodology it prescribes.

CLOSE THE TRUST GAP

Most organizations suffer from "The Trust Gap."

When asked, "Do you trust your manager?" 72 percent of employees answered "strongly agree." When asked, "Do you trust the senior leaders of your organization?" only 24 percent answered "strongly agree."

This 48 percent difference is a serious indictment of most senior executive teams.

Why don't employees trust executives? There are several reasons:

Many executive teams have extremely low trust *among their own team.* If they don't trust each other, why should anyone else trust them?

If one executive is the root of the problem, perhaps it is time for that person to go.

Many executive teams are isolated. They are literally "on mahogany row in the ivory tower."

Many executives have simply made decisions that made them untrustworthy. They lied to their employees. They cut corners. They cheated their partners. They scammed their vendors.

Building trust is a long-term process. It must be earned every day.

THE ONE PERCENTERS

Every organization recruits, develops, deploys, and rewards people. But in our experience, only one in a hundred organizations does this right.

We call them the "One Percenters."

Given the importance of having the right team, why is this so rare?

First, some organizations simply don't care about people. They might say the right words, but their actions don't back them up. They see people as an expense, not an investment. They focus on what they can get from people, not what they can give.

Second, some organizations care but don't have a system to develop a high-performance team. They pursue a haphazard mix of tactics but never really put all the pieces together.

Others care but simply underinvest in the process of developing people.

But the One Percenters make people development their number-one priority. They invest time, money, and energy to get the people side of their business right.

GOODWILL WRITEDOWN

In today's economy, many organizations have taken the perspective that "Our employees should stop complaining. They are lucky to even have a job."

Really?

These organizations have used the economy as an excuse for misguided management actions, such as:

- Reducing communications, especially regarding poor financial results or layoffs.

- Throwing temper tantrums, such as AN E-MAIL RANT ALL IN CAPS SENT BY THE CEO WHO IS PISSED OFF.

- Eliminating recognition, even though people are doing two or three jobs because of layoffs.

When the economy recovers, these organizations will discover a new meaning of the accounting term "goodwill writedown."

While the accountants do not have a specific entry for employee goodwill, it is a tremendously valuable asset.

Cultivate it, and your employees will reward you. Destroy it, and you'll be writing down your most important assets.

A SACRED TRUST

Over the course of my career, I have worked for more than 25 managers.

A few have been life-changingly horrible. Most have been okay. And a few have been astonishingly great.

The great ones cared about me as a person, not just as an employee. They invested in my development. And they pushed me hard ... really hard. And I'll never forget them.

These select few understood that managing people is a sacred trust.

They understood that they had the power to change the lives of the people who worked for them. For better... or worse.

Make a list of all the managers you have ever worked for.

Rank them from best to worst.

Pick up the phone and thank the best ones.

If you are like me, the worst ones did some real damage. Maybe you should call them too.

Forgiveness is a powerful thing.

BECOMING A GREAT MANAGER

If you are interested in becoming a great manager, there are five critical steps:

Step one is to decide that you really, really want to be a great manager.

(Surprisingly, a really small percentage of managers take this step.)

Step two is to approach your responsibility as a sacred trust.

Step three is to learn everything you can about managing people. Most organizations don't do any management training, so you'll most likely have to do this on your own.

Step four is to get to know your people really well. Learn about their unique strengths. Get to know their hopes and ambitions. Learn what makes them tick.

Step five is to develop a broad repertoire of management styles. Then, tailor your management style to each employee. Employees are unique, and your management style must be uniquely tailored to them.

Being a great manager is hard, which is why great managers are so rare. If you want to become one, follow these steps.

THE LONG UPHILL CLIMB

While the winners of the Best Places to Work awards celebrate, the losers are having a range of reactions.

Some organizations "sweep the results under the rug." They basically ignore the feedback, often using the excuse that the process is rigged.

Some react with anger and retribution. They are mad at the employees, and go into a rant, such as, "These people. After all I've done for them. $&#!?##!!"

A few will convene task forces to work on the issues identified by the survey. However, most will fade away and nothing will change.

The best organizations see the results as a wake-up call. They develop real action plans to improve.

In these organizations, the CEOs make employee engagement *their* number-one priority.

Getting to Best Place to Work levels is a long, uphill climb.

Most won't try. Some will try, but give up. A few—perhaps 1 percent of organizations—will make the commitment, invest the resources, stay the course, and reach the summit.

GETTING ENGAGED

To become differentiatingly great at One Thing, one thing is clear.

You need EVERY employee to get engaged.

It is tempting to think that improving engagement is primarily the job of the senior executives. However, in reality, it is everyone's responsibility.

Everyone contributes to the culture. When you tolerate behavior that is out of line, it reduces everyone else's engagement.

Everyone is a member of the team. When you disparage your teammates, it reduces everyone else's engagement.

Everyone has internal customers. When you miss deadlines or deliverables, it reduces everyone else's engagement.

Everyone owns the strategy. When you allow negativity and pessimism, it reduces everyone else's engagement.

Everyone has the choice of buying in or opting out. When you opt out, It reduces everyone else's engagement.

So, like so many other things in life, engagement is a choice.

TOP GEAR

My favorite television show is *Top Gear,* the hilarious car show on BBC.

Of course, whenever I watch the show, I try to make the connection to organizational performance.

So here it is: we don't just want employees to be engaged.

We want them engaged in Top Gear.

When leaders create demotivating environments, people respond by downshifting and working at a small fraction of their potential.

In contrast, top gear organizations create a culture that optimizes engagement.

When you put people first, employees respond by putting the organization first.

When commitment is appreciated, people go the extra mile.

When you inspire greatness, people dig deep.

When the expectation level is high, people rise to meet it.

Top gear is your organization's maximum efficiency.

DIAGNOSING UNDERPERFORMANCE

Every organization has underperformers.

But those that tolerate underperformance never reach their potential.

The first step is to understand the root cause of an employee's underperformance. You can't address the problem until you have diagnosed the root cause.

There are many reasons why people underperform:

Some people simply have no work ethic.

Some people are unmotivated. However, sometimes the organization has done things to demotivate the employee. So, you need to look at yourself also.

Some people are in the wrong job. Explore the possibility of moving them to a different role.

Some people lack the skills required. If people have a good work ethic and share your values, help them acquire the skills required to succeed.

Sometimes there is bad chemistry between the employee and the manager. Transfer that person to a different manager.

So, if you have someone who is not performing, do the diagnostic.

UNDERPERFORMANCE

MANAGEMENT

Confronting underperformers is difficult.

Therefore, most organizations avoid it, procrastinating the conversation in hopes that the problem will solve itself.

It rarely does.

We advise our clients to identify the bottom performers at the beginning of every quarter.

These underperformers are put on a 90-day improvement plan.

Then, at the beginning of the next quarter, we evaluate whether the employee has made the necessary improvements.

If not, the answer is clear: we must confront the issue.

We call this process "underperformance management."

WHAT TOOK THEM SO LONG?

Implementing underperformance management takes discipline and organizational will. But the benefits are substantial.

Everyone will thank you.

Your clients will thank you. In many cases, they have been on the receiving end of your employee's underperformance, and will probably be thinking, "What took them so long?"

Your star employees will thank you. They have been carrying the extra load, fixing the underperformer's mistakes. This can be a significant demotivator for high performers.

Your bottom line will thank you. In fact, you pay for underperforming employees three times. First, there is the cost of their salary and benefits. Then, there is the cost of their mistakes. Finally, there is the cost of paying someone else to fix their mistakes.

Often, the underperforming employee will thank you as well. After all, no one wants to work in a job that doesn't fit.

Finally, unless there is some serious ethical offense, it is important to treat people well on their way out.

Perhaps the Golden Rule should rule.

INVEST AND GROW

Recently, I was interviewing a CEO who *proudly* described his HR policy as "burn and churn." (What he meant was that he hires people, burns them up, and churns them out.)

Interestingly, this organization's revenues have been in a steady decline.

Do you think there is a correlation here? You bet.

Invest in the growth and development of your team, and they will invest their talents in the growth and development of your customers.

There is a running debate about which comes first, the customer or the employee.

Some argue, "The customer comes first."

Others argue, "The customer comes second. If you treat your employees well, they will serve your customers well."

Regardless of which of these you think is right, invest and grow beats burn and churn every time.

CLOSE THE CONTRIBUTION GAP

I often ask people a simple question: "Are you contributing at the absolute maximum of your potential?"

The vast majority of them will say no.

We call this the "contribution gap."

The contribution gap is the difference between employees' potential contribution and their actual contribution. This is potential that you are paying for but not getting. In most organizations this is big money.

Consider an organization with an average total compensation of $100,000 and a 10 percent contribution gap. That organization is paying someone $100,000/year but is only getting $90,000/year's worth of contribution.

At 100 employees, this represents $1 million per year!

Of course, people are responsible for their own behavior and actions. However, high-performance organizations create environments that allow people to flourish. They are exceptional at maximizing the contribution of every single employee.

High performers put people before profits...and ironically, that is exactly why they are so profitable.

ORANGE FLOWERS

I recently read some research from Gallup about employee engagement. Here's what the report stated:

"Seventy-one percent of American workers are 'not engaged' or 'actively disengaged' in their work, meaning they are emotionally disconnected from their work-places and are less likely to be productive."

In my experience, one of the key reasons that employees disengage is that they don't feel appreciated.

A simple thank you goes a long way. But a creative, unique, and differentiated thank you will never, ever be forgotten.

Like orange flowers.

One of our clients, BTI360, recently sent flowers to the spouse of a teammate who worked especially long hours to complete a critical project.

Sending flowers to a spouse will definitely go a long way.

But BTI360 did not just send flowers; they sent orange flowers (see the "One Color" story).

This was a creative, unique, and differentiated thank-you that will never, ever be forgotten.

ULTRA PREMIUM

I pulled into the neighborhood Sunoco to gas up the Porsche, and was faced with a decision.

Sunoco offers four choices, ranging from 87 octane at $3.80/gallon to 93 octane at $4.04/gallon.

Leaders face this same decision every day.

Employees "pull in to the station" to get refueled. They have been toiling in the marketplace to overcome obstacles, deliver results, and meet the ever-rising expectations set by their bosses.

Many are running on empty.

When thinking about their employees, many leaders reach for the low-grade fuel.

They give the minimum raise that they can get away with. They promise bonuses but then renege on paying them.

They reward someone who just delivered a multimillion dollar project with a $5 Starbucks card.

Leaders, if you want your people to perform at their best, treat them like Porsches.

Fill them with high-octane fuel.

A FOLLOWER WORTH LEADING

We challenge leaders to take a hard look at themselves to see if they are "a leader worth following."

But it is equally important to challenge followers with a similar question:

Are you "a follower worth leading?"

So, what makes someone a follower worth leading?

Great followers

- Accept (and implement) decisions that they did not help make

- Highlight their boss's strengths, rather than criticize their weaknesses

- Express concerns privately and directly rather than at the water cooler

- Demonstrate loyalty and respect

- Give the boss's initiatives their very best, even if they don't fully agree with them

- Keep their word, meet their deadlines, and make their numbers…not one time, but every time.

Great leaders are rare. But perhaps great followers are even rarer.

DEVELOP THE #ONE TEAM
AN ALIGNMENT CHECKLIST

Our *Decide One Thing. Align Everything. Win!* model provides a roadmap for creating a differentiating competitive advantage.

But it only works if you really do align everything and everyone.

Consider the following checklist as a starting point:

1. One Force (executive leadership)
2. One Structure
3. One Magnet (recruiting)
4. One On-Ramp (on-boarding)
5. One 101 (training)
6. One Package (compensation)
7. One Trophy (recognition)
8. One Voice (internal communications)
9. One Playbook
10. One Scale (performance ratings)

If you have aligned all ten of these elements of your human capital, you are probably on your way to the winner's circle!

DRIVE ONE
DIRECTION

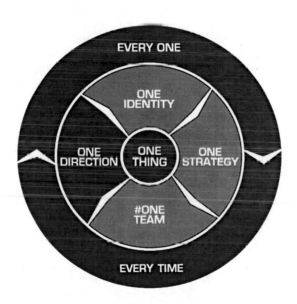

DRIVE ONE DIRECTION

Every organization is moving.

But most are moving in a hundred different directions.

In contrast, high performers apply intense management effort to drive their organizations in One Direction.

Fred Smith, CEO of FedEx, says, "Alignment is the essence of management."

Harvard Business School Professors Kaplan and Norton confirm this idea: "Alignment, much like the synchronism achieved by a high-performance rowing crew, produces dramatic benefits."

High-performance organizations know that fragmentation kills, and Drive One Direction to optimize their organizations to win.

So, is everyone in your organization driving in One Direction?

ONE DESTINATION

In our One Vision process, organizations determine their "SMART Vision."

Often this is a long-term revenue goal with a catchy slogan, such as "20 million by 2020."

SMART Visions are good, but they must be broken down into annual and quarterly goals that drive alignment.

In our experience, the process used to set the goals is more important than the goals themselves. (The right goal set with the wrong process will never have buy-in, and will therefore never be achieved.)

The One Destination process leverages four critical steps:

- Confronting reality
- Top-down forecast
- Bottom-up forecast
- Negotiation and finalization

In addition, the goals must be cascaded throughout the organization in the One Roadmap process.

This process goes a long way toward building ownership.

Remember, it is one thing to "assign" goals; it is another thing to have people own them.

ONE BUDGET

In most situations, there is a fixed amount of money that can be spent/invested in a year.

As a result, budget allocation decisions can be some of the most contentious ones in an organization.

Done poorly, this creates a zero-sum game with winners and losers.

Winners gloat and losers mope.

In high-performance organizations, the budgeting strategy is much more effective.

They have One Budget.

The One Thing idea is based on the premise that an organization has to be good at lots of things, but great at One Thing.

And becoming truly great at One Thing will take resources.

In fact, leaders must invest a disproportionate share of the organization's resources in their One Thing, leaving other initiatives funded to a "just- good-enough" level.

Being great takes more than lip service; it takes hard decisions.

TRACTION MANAGEMENT

My BMW has a very sophisticated all-wheel-drive traction management system. In any road condition, the car is unstoppably planted.

Traction is what converts RPM into MPH!

In many organizations, however, initiatives simply are not getting traction.

They have the pedal to the metal, but they just aren't getting anywhere.

Turbulent times and uncertain economic outlooks are the equivalent of icy winter storms.

To get to your destination, you'll need a sophisticated traction management system.

Without it, you'll just keep spinning your wheels.

Perhaps it is time to take a close look at your organization's strategy management system.

It is what converts strategy into results.

THE CONFUSED MIND
ALWAYS SAYS NO

Awhile back, I worked with a sales executive who cut his teeth in a hard-core, door-to-door, sales organization.

The company sold coupons for automotive repair services. Each rep would knock on hundreds of doors every day, facing mindboggling levels of rejection.

Although I have had hundreds of hours of sales training, he taught me something I had never heard before:

"The confused mind always says no."

The corollary for leaders is: "The confused organization always shifts into neutral."

So, if your organization has shifted into neutral, take a hard look at your management communications.

Are you clear? Consistent? Compelling?

Or confusing?

POTHOLES

Recently, I hit two huge potholes on the way home. It was dark, and I never even saw them coming. The force was enough to make me check if any of my teeth had been jarred loose!

And it was enough to knock my car out of alignment.

Organizations hit potholes too. Some are enough to knock the organization out of alignment, such as:

- The unexpected loss of a key executive, especially the CEO

- The unexpected loss of a major account

- Hiring a senior executive who is competent, but does not share the organization's values

- Reorganizations, especially ones that are not well planned

- Mergers, which fail to achieve their stated goals 75 percent of the time

- Failed new initiatives, especially ones that were sold as "essential to our future"

Hitting potholes takes its toll on the organization.

EMPLOYEE ALIGNMENT

Once an organization has decided on their One Thing, it is essential to bring everything—and everyone—into alignment with it.

Of course, it is far easier to align things than people.

To help leaders assess the alignment level of employees, SHIFTPOINTS developed the Employee Alignment model:

- **A-Players** are totally aligned, on-board, and engaged. These are your allies and ambassadors.

- **B-Players** are not convinced yet. They have some "buts." They are the right people, but they have not gotten on the bus!

- **C-Players** are the critics, complainers, and congenital naysayers. They have checked out.

- **CA-Players** are the change agents. There is a big difference between a change agent who challenges assumptions, and a C-Player who criticizes everything. The difference? Motive.

- **D-Players** are disgruntled, discouraged, disenfranchised, and demoralize everyone around them. You have to get them out ASAP.

Do the assessment. How many A-Players do you have?

TURBOCHARGED

My car is a twin turbocharged BMW.

In case you don't have a degree in automotive engineering, let me explain how a turbocharger works.

In a normal engine, gasoline is mixed with air and is then ignited by the spark plug to produce power.

The hot gasses left over from this process simply flow out the exhaust pipes into the environment.

A turbocharger is a small device that looks like a fan.

It "recycles" the hot exhaust gasses and forces them back into the engine.

It turns what would otherwise have been wasted into additional horsepower.

Alignment is the turbocharger of organizational performance.

The Drive One Direction process "recycles" the energy that is wasted by misalignment, and turns it into additional people power.

Enabling you to zoooooom past your competition!

BOTH AND

A long time ago a pastor introduced me to the phrase, "both and." This is something the grammarians call "paired conjunctions."

So, what does that have to do with building high-performance organizations?

More than you might think.

By now, you know that we are passionate about organizational alignment.

However, in today's turbulent world, it is essential to build an organization that is both aligned and agile.

Alignment without agility creates a slow, unresponsive bureaucracy, like a railway with 120 cars, all in a row.

But agility without alignment creates chaos, like lottery balls blown helter-skelter in a big glass bowl.

The goal is the best of both: aligned agility.

High-performance organizations keep these two (seemingly opposing) objectives in a dynamic tension.

RELATED...BUT DIFFERENT

For many, being with relatives during the holidays can be pretty stressful. Why?

Because you are related...but different.

You are related, which means that your DNA has some familial markers. You have common experiences.

But you are different. In most cases, very different!

You grew up in the same environment but now have totally different values. You have the same parents but now have opposing worldviews.

You used to be inseparable, but now barely speak.

Now, if it is hard for family members who are related to get along and work together, imagine just how challenging it is to ask *unrelated*...and very different people to come together and work as a team.

To do this, leaders must find common ground. Great leaders do it with such force, clarity, and intensity that unrelated and very different people come together as one.

That is why we use the word *One* over and over again.

So people can Drive in One Direction!

FASTER IS BETTER

There is an obvious lesson from the Indy 500,

Faster is better!

Every organization has dozens of internal processes and hand-offs. Hundreds of meetings. Countless forms. Endless e-mails.

To streamline operations and accelerate results, organizations should consider:

- Mapping every critical process to identify and eliminate wait times and redundancy.

- Analyzing the meeting schedule, eliminating those that are not absolutely essential.

- Making every meeting 50 percent shorter.

- Reducing the length of every form by 50 percent. Better yet, cut all of them down to one page!

- Writing shorter e-mails.

The cumulative effect of these—and dozens of other items—will make the entire organization faster.

And just like racing, faster is better.

DRIVE ONE DIRECTION
AN ALIGNMENT CHECKLIST

Our **Decide One Thing. Align Everything. Win!** model provides a roadmap for creating a differentiating competitive advantage.

But it only works if you really do align everything and everyone.

Consider the following checklist as a starting point:

1. One Destination
2. One Roadmap
3. One #One Priority
4. One Budget
5. One Dashboard
6. One Number
7. One System
8. One Calendar
9. One Standard
10. One Meeting

If you have aligned all ten of these elements of your management system, you are probably on your way to the winner's circle!

ACCELERATOR #6

DEVOTE
EVERY ONE

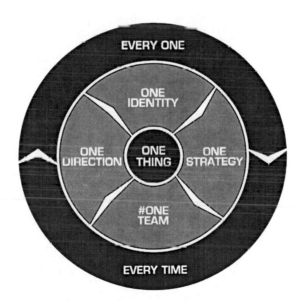

DEVOTE EVERY ONE

Every organization has people.

But most organizations don't engage EVERY ONE in the growth process.

In contrast, high performers Devote Every One in the organization to the process of serving clients and growing the business.

This starts with people in front-line, client-facing functions who interact with clients every day.

Likewise, marketing and sales must be optimized to communicate the benefits of the One Thing.

Great organizations extend this concept further and "connect the dots" with everyone, even those in support roles.

So, is every one of your people devoted to helping you grow?

THE FRONT LINE

Everyone in an organization is important. But external, customer-facing, value-delivering people are especially important.

They are your front line.

Everything that your front-line people say and do has a direct impact on revenue. Therefore, high performers ensure that they have the very best people in customer-facing roles.

In addition, high performers also make sure that their front line people have everything they need to deliver. This includes training, tools, technology, uniforms, trucks, collateral materials, and so on.

Recently, I encountered a front-line person who was "out of uniform." His hat was from a golf course. His jacket was from a vendor. His shirt had his company's old logo.

When I confronted him about the issue, I was shocked at the answer:

"They cut back on the clothing budget, and only the office people got the new stuff."

Amazing.

THE SUPPORTING CAST

It is critical for the "back office" departments within the organization to understand that they are in *supporting* roles.

Their job is to serve the customer by serving the people who serve the customer.

In some organizations, there is push-back from the support teams, whose members think this makes them "second-class citizens."

In the worst offenders, this manifests itself as resentment or even hostility.

In contrast, high performers don't fall for this reasoning and unashamedly give their front-line people special attention.

Align your front line with your customers.

Then, align your support team with your front line.

Every One is important. Every One has a role to play. Every One has an impact on customer satisfaction, retention and growth.

WHAT DOES TEAM MEAN?

A lot has been written about teamwork.

But most people have never been on a high-performance team. Thus, they do not have a real framework or experience base to work from.

They don't really know what "team" means.

In addition, there are many different kinds of teams:

A golf team is a loose collection of individuals, all playing their own games. The team wins if enough people play their individual matches well. However, it is possible for an individual to win the overall trophy, yet have his or her team lose the match.

A football team is an interdependent group of very diverse individuals, each of whom has very specialized skills. Some players weigh 380 pounds; others weigh 180. Some are fast; others are slow. Some kick, others throw.

A crew team, in contrast, is a much more homogeneous group. Each member has a virtually identical build and identical skill set. There is only one team, and they must work in perfect harmony in order to win. They are all in the same boat!

EVERYONE SELLS

If I asked you how many salespeople you have, what number would you use?

The right answer would be the number of employees you have.

High-performance organizations design a channel strategy that is aligned with their One Thing.

They utilize the appropriate mix of direct and indirect channels to serve their One Core Market. Channels are managed to optimize coverage and revenue while minimizing conflict and churn.

So far, so good.

We advise our clients to apply the "Everyone Sells" model.

At NeoSystems Corp. we translated this into what is called the "Five-Part Sales Model."

It starts with "Deliver and Delight" and ends with "Propose and Close."

This model has allowed Every One to find his or her place in the process.

ONE CHANNEL

It is great to have an Every One Sells culture.

But you will never win without a high-performance sales channel.

This process starts with your One Thing.

Then, we can design One Channel to sell it.

There are lots of questions that must be answered to design a high-performance sales channel, such as:

- What selling skills are required?

- What product knowledge is required?

- What is the sales process?

- How do we optimize efficiency?

- Should we go direct, indirect, or use a hybrid of multiple channels?

Organizations also debate lots of assumptions (and preconceived notions) about salespeople, such as hunters, farmers, account managers, and order takers.

The good news is that your One Thing will provide real clarity to address these issues.

WHAT BUSINESS ARE YOU IN?

I ask this question all the time.

People always say something like, "We are in the advertising business," or "We are in the software business."

In my opinion, these answers are wrong.

Regardless of what your business card says, you are in the PEOPLE business.

For most of our clients, the factor constraining their growth is not marketing, or sales, or business development.

It is people.

We now advise all of our clients with the following mantra, "You are in the people business. Your growth is constrained only by your ability to recruit, develop, inspire, and unleash the talents of great people."

Most leaders will say they agree with this. But only a few really mean it.

PROMISE POINTS

High-performance organizations are disciplined about their promises.

As our moms told us, we must keep our promises!

Most organizations have dozens of "promise points," including their:

- Website

- Advertising

- Marketing collateral

- Salespeople

- Sales proposals

- Customer service people

- And more

The route to failure is paved with broken promises.

When was the last time you took a hard look at all of the promises you are making? Are they really true?

If you are like most organizations, you have experienced significant "promise inflation."

Therefore, you must be very serious about sales integrity, and guard against the tendency to promise anything to get the deal.

AGGRESSIVE...OR DISHONEST?

In the competitive battlefield, organizations often have to push beyond their comfort zones to win.

But there is a fine line between being aggressive and being dishonest.

If you have been around the block as many times as I have, I'm sure you've seen them all:

- Ads that promise benefits that are simply untrue.

- Salespeople who promise dates that can't be met.

- Executives who fly in to "close the deal" and promise solutions that don't exist

What are you promising? How do you ensure that you don't promise more than you can deliver?

Is it even ethical to promise things that you know you can't deliver with the thought that you will figure out how to deliver it if we win the business?

There is a fine line between being aggressive and putting your best foot forward, and being unethical by lying about your capabilities.

ONE CAMPAIGN

To generate sales leads, you must develop One Campaign.

Because customers can't buy from you if they don't know you exist.

The Decide One Thing process provides much-needed clarity for your marketing campaign.

First, it makes the overall corporate value proposition crystal clear.

Second, it makes the target customer crystal clear as well.

As a result, organizations can generate the much-needed alignment between marketing and sales.

The marketing campaign is tuned to only generate leads from prospects that value your One Thing.

Of course, this takes discipline, because marketing will get pressure to glom up the message with all kinds of superfluous stuff.

Remember, trying to be all things to all people is the recipe for mediocrity.

THE NEW WORLD

I spent the first half of my life in sales. I spent the next half in marketing. I've spent the last half doing organizational development.

Now you know why I did not go into accounting!

This breadth of experience has given me a unique perspective on these functions.

One thing is certain; the world of marketing has totally changed.

The new world of marketing is driven by technology, and fueled by analytics.

The breadth of media outlets is mind-numbing. There are millions of websites, thousands of magazines, and thousands of TV channels.

Allocating the marketing budget has never been more complicated. Most companies are operating in multiple countries, communicating in multiple languages, selling multiple product lines.

The good news is that your One Thing provides the overall clarity required to create a compelling marketing campaign.

LEARNING FROM LOSING

Every day in the marketplace, hundreds of RFPs are being awarded. There are winners and losers.

Winners celebrate; losers commiserate.

In our experience, losing companies rarely do post-mortem loss reviews to find out why they lost.

Was it price? A missing product feature? Bad sales relationships? A poorly written RFP? Perhaps the client did not understand the value added differentiation? All of the above? None of the above?

Back in the early 1980s, when I was with IBM, the company had a very disciplined loss-review process that kicked in every time IBM lost a major sale.

It was an extremely intense experience for those sales reps who had the misfortune of going through it. (Fortunately, I never did...but I'll never forget the smell of burning flesh coming from the conference room!)

It is one thing to lose. It's another thing to not know why.

GAME FILMS AND BLACK BOXES

Jim Collins has a great phrase that describes the attitude that must prevail when conducting loss reviews.

Autopsies without blame.

The goal of a loss review is to deliver objective, actionable insight that allows our clients to improve sales performance.

- *Objective.* In particular, loss reviews must be done by an independent outside party with no agenda. SHIFTPOINTS provides an objective, outside perspective that will get to the real facts and lessons.

- *Actionable.* Our research is conducted with "learn-and-improve" rather than a "blame-and-fire" attitude. Final reports will contain specific recommendations for improvement based on specific customer feedback.

The result is that companies can dramatically improve sales performance by capturing lessons from lost sales and implementing changes required so that the same mistakes are not made again.

Sports teams study game films. The FAA analyzes black boxes. Winning sales teams conduct loss reviews.

DEVOTE EVERY ONE
AN ALIGNMENT CHECKLIST

Our *Decide One Thing. Align Everything. Win!* model provides a roadmap for creating a differentiating competitive advantage.

But it only works if you really do align everything and everyone.

Consider the following checklist as a starting point:

1. One Responsibility (everyone sells)

2. One Foundation (current customers)

3. One Campaign (marketing)

4. One Channel (sales organization)

5. One Funnel (pipeline)

6. One Carrot (sales compensation)

7. One Reason (sales collateral)

8. One Covenant (proposals)

9. One Conversation (price negotiations)

10. One Lesson (loss reviews)

If you have aligned all ten of these elements of your sales and marketing system, you are probably on your way to the winner's circle!

DELIVER
EVERY TIME

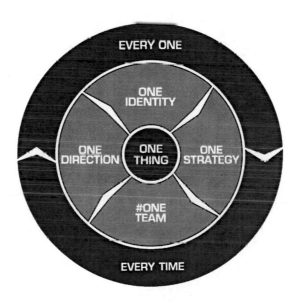

DELIVER EVERY TIME

Every organization makes promises.

But most don't actually keep them.

In contrast, high performance organizations promise exactly what they really deliver, and really deliver exactly what they promise.

Not one time, but EVERY TIME.

Every year, organizations spend billions in marketing, making promises to customers. To cut through the clutter and stand out from the competition, their claims get bigger and more audacious.

Every day, salespeople make promises to customers. To win the deal, their promises get bolder and more exaggerated.

And customers make purchase decisions based on these heightened promises. Too often, what they actually experience is a far cry from what the organization promised.

We call this the "Customer Experience Gap" and it is a root cause of slow growth, poor profitability, and low morale.

So, how big is your Customer Experience Gap?

WHERE THE RUBBER
MEETS THE ROAD

Promising One Thing is one thing. Delivering it Every Time is another thing!

This is where the rubber meets the road.

Obviously, the process starts with clarifying exactly what you are promising.

You must also really understand what your customers are expecting.

Sometimes, they are expecting things that you are not aware of. Sometimes, they are expecting things that they could not have articulated in advance.

Once you have clarified your promise and your customer's expectations, you can optimize the delivery process.

Process optimization must focus on reducing variability so that the organization can indeed deliver what you promise every time.

In our experience, simplification is the key.

We advise our clients to make things easy to sell, easy to buy, and easy to deliver.

But as Apple says so eloquently on its website, "Simplicity isn't simple."

MORTONS AND MCDONALDS

We have all been victimized by vendors who overpromise and underdeliver.

We call it, "Promising Mortons and delivering McDonalds."

I experienced this recently when I hired a landscaping company whose ads promised results that would be "picture perfect every time."

Being a recovering perfectionist, this was extremely appealing to me.

I won't go in to the details, but suffice it to say that I would NEVER work with them again.

Unfortunately, this is all too common.

An accounting firm won over one of my clients by promising to overhaul my client's business operations.

My client fired the firm 90 days later for overpromising and underdelivering.

Some organizations could use a "promise management system" to keep track of everything they have promised.

Others could use a serious reality check.

ONE WOW!

You have purchased thousands of things in your life.

How many times have you said, "WOW!"?

Once you have Decided One Thing, you can begin the process of designing One WOW!

Consider the process of checking into a hotel.

If Ritz Carlton and Motel 6 compiled their "moments of truth," the lists would be very similar.

However, the customer experience could not be more different. Which is exactly how it should be.

Why?

Because they have radically different promises.

The Ritz Carlton wants to WOW! you with service.

Motel Six wants to WOW! you by leaving the light on.

In most cases, it does not really take that much to WOW! your customers. But it does take intentionality.

You must select One moment of truth and overexecute so amazingly that customers can only say one thing: "WOW!"

DELIVER EVERY TIME
AN ALIGNMENT CHECKLIST

Our *Decide One Thing. Align Everything. Win!* model provides a roadmap for creating a differentiating competitive advantage.

But it only works if you really do align everything and everyone.

Consider the following checklist as a starting point:

1. One Front-Line

2. One Support Team

3. One Experience (customer experience)

4. One Hundred Percent (delivery)

5. One Process (simplification)

6. One WOW!

7. One Validation

8. One Ring (service)

9. One Question (customer satisfaction)

10. One Bill

If you have aligned all ten of these elements of your delivery system, you are probably on your way to the winner's circle!

SUMMARY

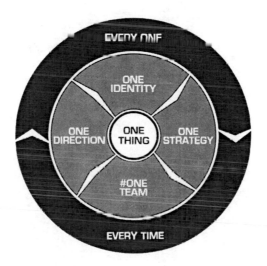

THE LAST 1,000 FEET

It was another wild finish at the 2011 Indy 500.

Dan Wheldon won after rookie J. R. Hildebrand crashed—in sight of the checkered flag—on the very last turn.

A 500-mile race translates into 2,640,000 feet. Dan Wheldon led just 1,000 of them. They just happened to be the 1,000 feet that mattered.

So, perhaps the hundredth running of the Indy 500 is a good reminder about what it takes to win.

Thirty-three teams started the race. All had hopes of winning. All worked extremely hard. Many had real chances. But in the end, it was Wheldon who made that famous "fifth left turn" and drank the milk.

This book is about shift points. It is designed for Fast Lane Leaders who want to break through plateaus and shift their organization's performance to a higher level.

We have covered 100 specific ideas. Each will help you shift your thinking and accelerate your results.

Taken individually, each idea can be a catalyst for your organization. Taken holistically, they represent a comprehensive roadmap that will shift your performance into top gear.

Succeeding in today's turbulent world is a bit like competing in the Indy 500. There will be crashes and disappointments. Engines will blow up. Drivers will make mistakes. Teams will run out of gas. Tires will blow.

In the end, one team will win. I hope it is you.

NOTE: Since this was originally written, Dan Wheldon was killed in a tragic crash at the 2011 IZOD IndyCar World Championship at Las Vegas Motor Speedway on October 16, 2011, at the age of 33. Our condolences go out to Dan's family, friends, and the entire Indy Racing League community.

MORE SHIFTPOINTS

We've all joked about the crazy late-night infomercials that try to sweeten the deal with the famous line, "But wait, there's more!!!"

In this book we promised to give you 100 ideas that would help improve the performance of your organization.

But in the spirit of delivering more than we have promised, here is one more idea to help you shift your thinking and accelerate your results:

Subscribe to the SHIFTPOINTS blog.

We post new ideas every Monday morning. You can read them online, or subscribe to them via e-mail or RSS.

Like the book, we cover a wide range of topics, from differentiation to winning, from strategy development to talent management.

The blog is written in the same punchy style as the book. Postings are designed to be read in 60 seconds.

Otherwise known as One Minute!

Fast. Informative. Provocative. And hopefully entertaining.

www.SHIFTPOINTS.com/blog

THE ULTIMATE SHIFT POINT

In the 1997 Indy 500, Arie Luyendyk was the fastest qualifier, at 218.263 miles per hour, which earned him the coveted pole position. Arie was fast all day, led 61 of the 200 laps, and went on to win the race, just 0.7 seconds ahead of his teammate Scott Goodyear.

It was an exciting day for Team Nortel, with our cars finishing first and second. When Arie drank the milk, I was standing just a few feet away. It was an unbelievable experience celebrating with the entire team.

Winning the race is great…but it is critical to choose the right race.

There are lots of races to choose from.

Some are focused on the race to the top, and define winning by their title.

Some are focused on the race for wealth, and define winning by their net worth.

Others are focused on the race for fame, and define winning by how many Twitter followers they have.

After many years running these races, I came to the Ultimate Shift Point. I was redlined, and knew that I was running the wrong race.

I was in the fast lane on the road to nowhere.

God intervened and illuminated my path. He showed me the way. He introduced me to His Son.

This led to a complete transformation of my goals, priorities, and worldview. I redefined success and now live with an eternal perspective. I'm on a different road, running a different race for different reasons. At the end of my race, I look forward to that "fifth left turn" into Jesus' presence.

For me, it was the Ultimate Shift Point.

ALSO BY DAVE RAMOS

ABOUT THE AUTHOR

Dave Ramos is the founder and CEO of SHIFTPOINTS, Inc.

Prior to founding SHIFTPOINTS, Dave built differentiation-driven organizations in a broad range of settings, including large global corporations, venture-backed start-ups, and innovative nonprofits.

He held executive positions with global leaders like Nortel Networks, where he was the Vice President of global marketing. At Nortel, Dave won the company's highest award, The Chairman's Award, for innovations in marketing. At IBM, Dave won the company's highest award, The Golden Circle, for innovations in sales.

He was employee #13 at AnswerLogic, a venture-backed software company, where he led sales, marketing, and business development.

After AnswerLogic, Dave spent four years doing pro bono consulting, volunteer work, and teaching.

One of his consulting clients, McLean Bible Church (a 15,000 person megachurch) asked him to join the staff full time. Surprising everyone, Dave accepted the job. He spent three years as the Director of Adult Ministries and led the church through a strategic alignment initiative.

He left the MBC staff to start The Dashboard Group, which changed its name to SHIFTPOINTS in January, 2013.

Dave has an MBA from the Harvard Business School and a BS in accounting from Drexel University. He serves on the Board of Directors for Fellowship of Christian Athletes Golf Ministry and Workforce Ministries.

Dave is a sought-after speaker, and engages audiences with his humorous yet challenging style. He has spoken at organizations such as The Harvard Business School, Nyack College, Vistage, Convene, The CXO Forum, AOL, and many churches and ministries around the country.

Dave is good at a lot of things, but is working to become differentiatingly great at his One Thing.

CPSIA information can be obtained at www.ICGtesting.com
Printed in the USA
BVOW02s0258140114

341804BV00016B/282/P